A BRIEF HISTORY OF THE MARYBOROUGH MARKETS

Compiled by
Rotary Club of Maryborough-Sunrise

© 2024

Published by Mary River Press Services

Thank you to the Fraser Coast Regional Council's Community Grants program for providing $920.00 to Rotary Club of Maryborough-Sunrise towards the Maryborough Markets 35 years – an Oral History project.

TABLE OF CONTENTS

Chapter One: Introduction: Birth of a Tradition...................................1

Chapter Two: Characters and Performers 4

Chapter Three: Organisations and Activities............................... 15

Chapter Four: Current and Future 22

Recommended Reading.. 26

Chapter One

INTRODUCTION: BIRTH OF A TRADITION

In November of 1987, the picturesque streets of Maryborough overseen by CEO Noel Gorrie, welcomed a new event that has become a central part of life in Maryborough. The opening of Coles Plaza Shopping Centre resulted in the exodus of shoppers from the Central Business District of Maryborough. Loretta Bertoldo-Hyne suggested to the Maryborough Promotions Bureau that a European style street market be established to bring people back to the city centre.

A survey charted the pulse of business, revealing Thursday as the quiet haven amid the week's hustle. Thus, Maryborough Heritage Market was born - a joyous response to the town's ebb and flow. Inspired by neighbouring Eumundi Markets, Thursday became a canvas for stall holders, seamlessly transitioning from Eumundi's Wednesday buzz. The streets were closed to vehicles and the Maryborough Markets began.

At the same time the vision emerged of Maryborough as a Heritage City, and with it, the birth of a beloved symbol: Mary Heritage. This character was conceived to embody the historical tapestry of a town that had been a key player in the history of Australia.

Step into Maryborough's past at the Markets. Discover the faces and stories behind the stalls, living embodiments of the town's history. Join the celebration of a tradition born and evolved — the Maryborough Markets and the vibrant characters who bring history to life.

A BRIEF HISTORY OF THE MARYBOROUGH MARKETS

(Image supplied by Gould Marketing)

Chapter Two

CHARACTERS AND PERFORMERS

The Maryborough Markets were visited by many characters. In 1989, the Ancient and Honourable Guild of Australian Town Criers was formed and Reg Lade became Maryborough's first official town crier and the custodian of the Time Cannon.

Reg Lade *(Image supplied by Ken Ashford)*

A BRIEF HISTORY OF THE MARYBOROUGH MARKETS

Olds and Sons created a replica of Maryborough's cannon, the original harking back to 1878 when Maryborough was a village of about 1000 people that lacked a clock and needed the cannon to keep the time. The cannon's thunderous proclamation at one o'clock Thursday, on Adelaide Street became a symbol of Maryborough's timeless tradition and you can still meet the Town Crier and hear the firing on the Town Hall Green on Thursday at 1pm.

Setting off the Time Cannon at the Town Hall Green with Reg Lade
(Image supplied by Carmel Murdoch)

Prior to 2004 Steve Battye assisted Reg before becoming Crier for the Shires of Woocoo, Tiaro and Hervey Bay.

Steve Battye *(Image supplied by Steve Battye)*

A BRIEF HISTORY OF THE MARYBOROUGH MARKETS

In 2004 Ken Ashford became Reg's assistant.

Ken Ashford *(Image supplied by Ken Ashford)*

As Reg's health failed, he became less active in the role and remained in the guild till his passing in 2009 often doubling as Santa Claus for the Christmas Markets. When Maryborough amalgamated with surrounding areas in 2008, Ken Ashford became the Official Town Crier for the Fraser Coast Regional Council. Prime Ministers and Miss Australia were among visitors invited to fire the Time Cannon.

Ken Ashford holds a cherished memory of a particular stall holder from the past. He warmly recalls, "There was a stall holder named Wolf who specialised in selling leather belts, and he had a husky dog. His stall was set right outside Boys (now Dimmeys)." Ken reminisces, "Wolf shared with me, when he was just a five-year-old, that his uncle used to be the Town Crier. Unfortunately, his uncle lost an arm, so Wolf stepped in to hold the bell. It's the closest thing to a real town crier I knew." Ken still volunteers his time.

A BRIEF HISTORY OF THE MARYBOROUGH MARKETS

Setting off the Time Cannon
(Image supplied by Carmel Murdoch)

Mary Heritage assisted with the cannon also. Mary Heritage, a figure rooted in the essence of Maryborough's past, found its first representative in the poised and charismatic Del Jensen. In her inaugural appearance, adorned in a taffeta dress and wig, and armed with a parasol, Del became the face of Mary Heritage during the illustrious World Expo 88. Little did the city know that this was the genesis of a tradition that would weave itself into the fabric of Maryborough's identity. John Craig Gardner, Mayor Ron Peters, and Alan Brown, Deputy Mayor lent their support, underscoring the importance of preserving Maryborough's unique history.

The mantle of Mary Heritage passed through the hands of individuals who not only played a role but became integral chapters in the town's historical saga. Barbara Barringhaus, taking on the role in 1989, brought with her a sartorial transformation, accurately depicting the attire of ladies from the 1850s. Following in her footsteps, Marjorie Green assumed the role for the next two years, leaving an indelible mark on the character.

Carmel Murdoch was appointed as Mary Heritage in February 1998. A custodian of the town's history, Carmel not only held the role for 23 years but elevated it to new heights. Her enduring commitment is evident in her participation in numerous Australian Town Criers' Championships, where she has been adorned with the accolade of Best Dressed Attendant of a Town Crier multiple times. Mary Heritage looked after lost children and made announcements on the microphone and doubled as Mary Christmas for the Christmas markets.

A BRIEF HISTORY OF THE MARYBOROUGH MARKETS

Town Criers' Championship Event *(Image supplied by Carmel Murdoch)*

The markets cannot be discussed without mentioning one of the longest serving stall holders Wayne and Sharon Usher 1987 to 2021 and the shop that has been in business the longest, Bill and Joan Langer's shoe business on Adelaide Street. Langers has been serving Maryborough since January 1926. Many of the current stallholders have attended the Maryborough Markets for many years and are still attending.

A BRIEF HISTORY OF THE MARYBOROUGH MARKETS

Langers Shoe Store *(Image supplied by Kathy Shilvock)*

ROTARY CLUB OF MARYBOROUGH-SUNRISE

The markets, an inclusive stage for diverse performers, included the talents of Simon Gallagher, Ken Clee, John Vea Vea and Frank Benn. Their performances added colourful strokes to the canvas of Maryborough, showcasing the town's dynamic spirit.

Chapter Three

ORGANISATIONS AND ACTIVITIES

Initially governed by the Maryborough Promotions Bureau under the sponsorship of the Maryborough City Council, the market's administration witnessed a shift post-amalgamation. The Fraser Coast Regional Council staff assumed control before passing the torch to Fraser Coast Opportunities, followed by Fraser Coast Tourism and Events. In a noteable shift, the managerial reins transitioned to Fraser Coast Rotary Events Inc, a not-for-profit organisation comprising members from the Rotary Club of Hervey Bay City and Rotary Club of Maryborough-Sunrise. This transfer of authority took effect in January 2022.

Initially the market was in Adelaide Street between Ellena and Kent Streets and in Kent Street between Adelaide and Bazaar Street. After 11 years, there were lots of complaints about the closure of Kent Street. To address concerns and explore new opportunities, the market relocated to Ellena Street, aiming to draw shoppers seamlessly from Station Square to Adelaide Street. In 2020, a temporary move to Macdowell Carpark demonstrated adaptability, reflecting the market's commitment to community service and an evolving retail landscape.

All the shops were encouraged to put their equipment on the street, with exercise equipment, knick knacks, clothes and food amongst the rich offerings. It was determined the markets offer a large range of stalls with an amazing array of farm fresh produce and unique wares, original hand-made craft, homemade treats, artwork, jewellery, clothing, accessories, natural beauty products and gorgeous cut flowers. No poor-quality second-hand items were to be for sale.

A BRIEF HISTORY OF THE MARYBOROUGH MARKETS

Carmel Murdoch and the Pharmacist dressed in costume for the Sports Expo theme day *(Image supplied by Carmel Murdoch)*

Market raffles *(Image supplied by Carmel Murdoch)*

The markets had lots of theme days Carmel Murdoch remembers "I worked in a pharmacy in Kent Street and the first one was Heritage Week, and the staff wore big dresses, and I went as a convict and was so disappointed when I discovered that all my ancestors were free settlers! Another theme was a Sport Expo, and I am pictured wearing my son's cricket pads and cap posing with a pharmacist on the street."

Other theme days include Christmas, Easter, Australia Day, Anzac Day, Naidoc Week, Mothers'/Fathers' Day, Mary Poppins, and the celebration of Spring. The first Mary Poppins market, inspired by the non-profit group Proud Marys' revitalisation of P.L. Travers connection with Maryborough, was held in 1999.

Regular theme days have returned to the Markets, alongside quality local entertainers that grace the Town Hall Green. People flock to enjoy the free music and soak in the delightful ambience each week.

A BRIEF HISTORY OF THE MARYBOROUGH MARKETS

Celebrating P.L. Travers birthday *(Image supplied by Carmel Murdoch)*

ROTARY CLUB OF MARYBOROUGH-SUNRISE

Maryborough Markets beach day theme
(Image supplied by Carmel Murdoch)

A BRIEF HISTORY OF THE MARYBOROUGH MARKETS

Maryborough Markets have seen a mix of community events. Fraser Coast Libraries present monthly literacy-focused storytelling sessions as well as activities for the younger crowd during Under Eight Week. One fondly recollected event is when Flipside Circus brought an extra dimension to the library events with hula hoops, human pyramids, clowning, acrobatics, diabolo, and devil sticks. Other events include orchestral showcases by school children on the Green, xylophone players, the animal refuge highlighting local initiatives, while the presence of the Police, SES, and Fire Brigade emphasises community safety education. Guided Heritage Walking tours and rides in the Mary Ann, a replica steam engine, all complement the market experience. Each event adds a piece to Maryborough's communal history, representing a diverse and engaging community gathering.

(Image supplied by Carmel Murdoch)

Chapter Four

CURRENT AND FUTURE

Fraser Coast Rotary Events Inc has revitalised the Maryborough Markets, bringing quality entertainment to a full market, that now includes stalls on the Town Hall Green. The organisation is considering linking with bus groups that attend the Brolga Theatre. A robust social media presence and community engagement amplify their impact. Funds raised are reinvested into the local community. Projects supported include empowering individuals with disabilities to launch microbusinesses based on their interests, community flights for patient transportation to and from Brisbane, and providing fully kitted backpacks for school children. Markets run Thursdays, from seven in the morning to midday, featuring gourmet food, unique clothing, handmade crafts, fresh produce, and more.

A BRIEF HISTORY OF THE MARYBOROUGH MARKETS

(Image supplied by Gould Marketing)

Thank you

Carmel Murdoch, Ken Ashford and Steve Battye for sharing their recollections of the markets and images included in this publication.

Gould Marketing for sharing images included in this publication.

Robyn Dowling and Kathy Shilvock, members of the Rotary Club of Maryborough-Sunrise, for contributions to the interviewing, compiling, formatting, publishing, grant application, and acquittal for this booklet.

A BRIEF HISTORY OF THE MARYBOROUGH MARKETS

(Image supplied by Gould Marketing)

RECOMMENDED READING

Lunney, G. (1990). *Heritage with a Bang*. New Life Press.

Hunter, J. R. (2005). *City of Maryborough, Queensland: 100 Years: 1905-2005*. Wise Owl Research Publishing.

A BRIEF HISTORY OF THE MARYBOROUGH MARKETS

Visit www.frasercoastrotaryevents.com.au, facebook.com/mbmarkets for details.

Join the markets for local flavours and new and familiar faces.

ROTARY CLUB OF MARYBOROUGH-SUNRISE

(Image supplied by Gould Marketing)

www.ingramcontent.com/pod-product-compliance
Lightning Source LLC
Chambersburg PA
CBHW042045290426
44109CB00001B/36